DRS ERNEST AND HAZEL LUCAS

Our World

Designed by Graham Round

A LION BOOK

Tring · Belleville · Sydney

Text copyright© 1986 Ernest and Hazel Lucas
This illustrated edition copyright© 1986 Lion Publishing

Lion Publishing Corporation
10885 Textile Road, Belleville, Michigan 48111, USA
ISBN 0 85648 948 4
Lion Publishing plc
Icknield Way, Tring, Herts, England
ISBN 0 85648 948 4
Albatross Books Pty Ltd
PO Box 320, Sutherland, NSW 2232, Australia
ISBN 0 86760 804 8

First edition 1986

Acknowledgments
Our thanks to Dr Anne Ramkaran for her help and advice
on biological matters.

Photographs by Andes Press Agency/Carlos Reyes 19 (children), 20 (food distribution); Barnaby's
Picture Library 12 (folded rocks); Tony Deane 20 (roadside clinic); Sonia Halliday Photographs 9
(astronaut); Eric and David Hosking 14; Frank Lane Agency/S. McCutchean 2; Lion
Publishing/David Alexander 19 (rubbish); NASA 3; Planet Earth Pictures/Geoff du Feu 6 (pond
skater) and 18 (bee)/J. & G. Lythgoe 7 (sunflowers)/David Maitland 9 (frost)/Dick Clarke 18
(divers)/Munesuke Yamamoto 19 (panda)/Menuhin 19 (penguin); Mick Rock 12 (Bryce Canyon);
Science Photo Library/R. Royer 4/Paul Shambroom 5 (observatory); Philip Selby 17 (boy on bike);
ZEFA 5 (galaxy), 6 (protozoa), 7 (cell), 11, 13, 16, 17 (child with newts).

Illustrations by Fred Apps 2 (core of the earth), 3 (planets), 16 (tube); Peter Cornwell 7 (plant cell),
13 (wings/arms); Peter Dennis 15 (dinosaurs), 16 (woolly mammoth); Vic Granger 14 (dogs); Brian
Green 20 (children); Annie Russell 13 (kangaroo); Michael Stringer 14 (finches). All other
illustration by Graham Round and Kim Blundell.

The two poems, 'Silence' on 18 and 'There is a dragon inside me' on 19 are from *Cadbury's
Second Book of Children's Poetry*, published by Arrow Books and reproduced by kind permission.

Library of Congress Cataloguing-in-Publication Data
Lucas, Ernest.
    Our world: how? what? when? why?
    'A Lion book.'
    Includes index.
    1. Earth—Juvenile literature. 2. Cosmology—
Juvenile literature. 3. Creation—Juvenile literature.
[1. Cosmology. 2. Creation] I. Lucas, Hazel.
II. Round, Graham, ill. III. Title.
QB631.L78 1986   523.1   86—2702
ISBN 0 85648 984 4

Printed in Belgium

CONTENTS

PLANET EARTH

Planet Earth . . . is our home in space. It is a spinning, rocky ball moving endlessly around the Sun.

A thin layer of air, called the atmosphere, surrounds the Earth. Oceans and seas cover nearly three-quarters of its surface.

Without water, air, and the light and heat that comes from the Sun there would be no life on Earth.

A force called gravity holds down the air, the oceans and everything else on the Earth – otherwise they would all drift away into outer space.

In between the Poles and the Tropics are the Temperate regions, which do not get as cold or as hot.

The Equator

The Equator is an imaginary line around the middle of the Earth, halfway between the North and South Poles. It divides the Earth in half. The top half is called the northern hemisphere and the bottom half the southern hemisphere.

The distance around the Earth at the equator is about 40,000km (25,000 miles). A car travelling at 80km/h (50 mph) would take about 3 weeks to go around it without stopping.

THE WATERY PLANET

The Earth is awash with water. A view of the Earth with Tahiti at its center shows that the Pacific Ocean, the largest of the oceans, covers nearly half the Earth's surface.

The average depth of the oceans is 4km (2.5 miles), much greater than the average land height, which is less than 1km (0.5 mile).

The floors of the oceans are not flat, but are a mysterious underwater world of submerged mountain ranges, valleys and plains. In some places the mountains stick up out of the ocean as islands.

In some parts of the ocean there are strong currents, as the warm water from the Tropics spreads north and south, and cold water from the Poles moves to replace it. The currents have an important effect on the weather, and on the life to be found in the water. Most of the life of the oceans is found in the top 100m (300ft) because little sunlight gets beyond this depth, but a few strange creatures do live in the cold and darkness lower down.

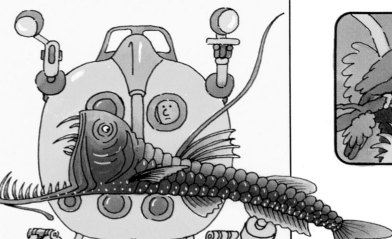

Near the Equator it is hot all year round. The hottest parts of the Earth are on either side of the Equator and are called the Tropics.

The further you live from the Equator the colder it is. The regions around the Poles are the coldest places on Earth and are always covered with ice. The Arctic is the area around the North Pole, and the region around the South Pole is called the Antarctic.

HOW HIGH IS THE SKY?

The Earth's atmosphere is a mixture of gases – mainly oxygen and nitrogen. We need the oxygen in order to breathe. It is impossible to say where the atmosphere ends. It just gets thinner as we go further away from the Earth's surface.

About nine-tenths of the air is found within 12km (8 miles) of the surface. This layer is called the Troposphere and it is here that clouds are formed. They are made of tiny droplets of water or crystals of ice.

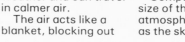

Most airplanes on long flights fly above the Troposphere, in the region called the Stratosphere. This means that they are above clouds and weather and can travel in calmer air.

The air acts like a blanket, blocking out some of the Sun's heat during the day so that the Earth does not get too hot, and keeping in the warmth by night so that it does not become too cold.

Compared with the size of the Earth the atmosphere is as thin as the skin on an apple!

MOON PROJECT

The Moon is a ball of rock which orbits around the Earth at a distance of 384,000km (238,000 miles), and is roughly one-quarter the size of the Earth. It has no atmosphere and is dry and lifeless. Without a protective blanket of air, the temperature rises to over 100°C (212°F) in the sunshine, and falls to 150°C below freezing (−240°F) on the dark side.

Here is a simple experiment you can do to show how the crescent moon becomes a full moon.

1 Set up a flashlight at eye level in a darkened room. Stand in front of it with one arm stretched out at head height. Rest a ball, such as a tennis ball, in the palm of your hand. Only half the ball will be lit by the torch, in the same way that only half the Moon is lit by the Sun.

2 Start with the ball held in line between you and the flashlight. Turn around slowly on the spot, holding the ball in your outstretched hand.

3 First you will see only a crescent of it lit up.

After a quarter of a turn, half of the ball will appear lit up.

4 When you have turned half-way around, the ball will be on the opposite side of you from the flashlight. All of it will appear lit up – like the full moon.

5 Now hold the ball exactly in line with your head and the flashlight. It will be in the shadow from your head and so not be lit up properly. This is like an eclipse of the Moon – it passes into the shadow of the Earth when it is on the opposite side of the Earth from the Sun and in line with them.

The spinning Earth

The Earth spins like a top about an imaginary line, called its 'axis,' which joins the North and South Poles.

It is this spinning which causes day and night, as first one side of the Earth and then the other faces the Sun. It takes 24 hours to go around once.

Because of its spin the Earth is not perfectly round but bulges a little at the Equator.

The distance through the Earth from the North Pole to the South Pole is about 40km (25 miles) less than that through the Earth at the Equator.

INSIDE THE EARTH

We live peacefully on the outer skin of our planet, and every day it seems just the same as the day before. But sometimes news of an earthquake or a volcano reaches the headlines of the world's papers. Then we are reminded that the Earth is not as quiet as it seems.

Just what is going on under our feet?

The Earth's crust: eggshell-thin

The outer layer of the Earth is made of tiny grains of crushed rock and the rotting remains of plants. Underneath that are layers of rock. You can sometimes see the layers on a cliff face, or a road or rail cutting. All our caves and mines are within these rocks. No one has ever dug below them.

The thickness of the Earth's **crust** varies from about 5km (3 miles) in some places to more than 50km (30 miles) in others. The thin places are under the ocean floor. Since the distance to the center of the Earth is 6400km (4000 miles), the Earth's crust, by comparison, is as thin as the shell on an egg.

Suppose you had a marvelous machine in which you could travel down to the center of the Earth. You would need a heat shield to prevent you from being boiled alive, and strong walls to withstand the enormous pressure.

Under the crust you would come to the **mantle**, a thick layer of dense, soft rock. The mantle is mostly solid, but there are regions where volcanic lava is formed. It gets hotter and softer as you go deeper. The mantle is 2900km (1800 miles) thick.

The Earth's **core** is very hot and very dense. The outer core is a red-hot liquid layer, 2100km (1300 miles) thick, and in the very center is a white-hot solid mass, 2800km (1700 miles) in diameter. The core may be made of metals such as iron or nickel, since they are very dense, but it could be other materials squashed into strange forms by the tremendous pressure and heat. The temperature at the center is not known exactly, but it is likely to be several thousand degrees Celsius. The pressure is more than 3 million atmospheres!

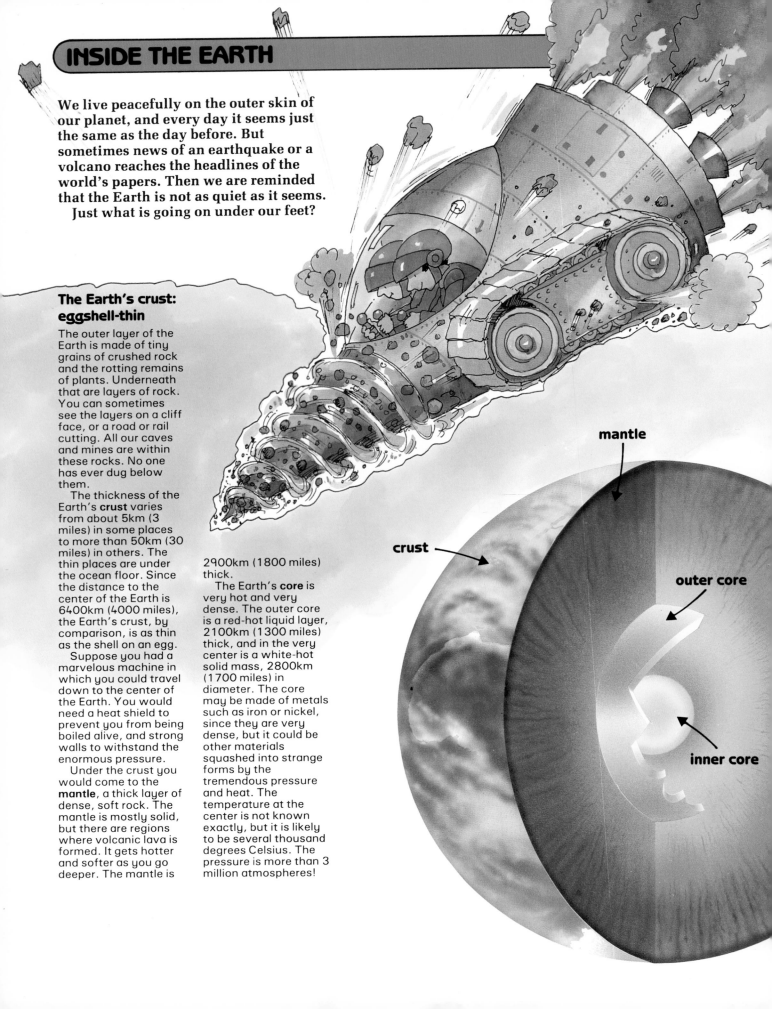

mantle

crust

outer core

inner core

Earthquake damage in Alaska.

Everything on the move

The liquid outer core is continually moving as the Earth spins, and these currents make the Earth into a giant magnet, attracting the needle of a compass to the north. There are other, slower movements as well, as great masses of rock are pulled and pushed about by different forces. The Earth's crust is floating on moving masses, so it is not surprising that places on the Earth's surface move too, perhaps 4cm (1½in.) in a year! The pyramids in Egypt have moved 4km (2.5 miles) since they were built in ancient times. Places can move up or down as well as sideways. Finland is rising, and the area around London, England, is sinking.

A map of the world, with active volcanoes and recent earthquakes marked on it, shows us what is happening. The Earth's surface can be divided up into six or seven large pieces which are slowly moving past each other. Earthquakes and volcanoes happen along the lines between two pieces.

Shockwaves through the Earth

An earthquake happens when huge masses of rock are pushed past each other and suddenly give way. Tremendous shock waves travel through the Earth and whole towns are sometimes destroyed. Scientists can use the waves to tell them where the earthquake started and the type of material through which the wave travelled. Scientists in different parts of the world take measurements and compare their results. Sometimes small explosions are caused deliberately to bounce shock waves off the various layers. In this way, even without going there, a picture of the center of the Earth has been built up.

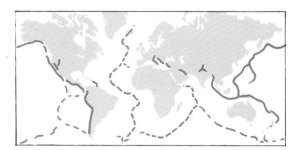

A GIANT JIGSAW

After the first explorers had travelled around the world, early map-makers noticed that the coasts of West Africa and South America seem to fit together like the pieces of a jigsaw. Since then it has been found that the older layers of rock on the two coasts match exactly. Millions of years ago, all the continents of the world were joined together, but they have been pushed apart by movements deep inside the Earth.

Perhaps you can work out where they are going next!

THE SUN'S FAMILY

Mercury

Venus

Our Earth is one of nine planets which go around the Sun, forming a family called the Solar System.

Five of these planets have been known for thousands of years because we can see them quite easily without a telescope.

The word 'planet' means wanderer because, although the planets look like stars, if we watch them night after night we can see that they move against the background of the stars, which are much further away. The movements follow a regular pattern, as the planets circle the Sun.

Earth

How did it all begin?

Astronomers think that the Solar System started as a spinning cloud of gas and dust. The particles attracted each other and moved closer together and, as they did so, the cloud spun faster. The center became a dense ball of hot gas, the Sun, surrounded by a flat ring of gas and dust around its equator. The planets formed within this flat ring.

If this idea is right, the Earth would have begun as a cold mass of dust, ice and gas. As it contracted under the force of gravity, and heat was given out by radioactive materials, it would warm up. There are signs that the Earth was once molten and has cooled down to become as it is today. Many people believe that God created planet Earth. This theory may tell us the method he used.

Mars

Asteroids

THE INNER PLANETS

The four planets nearest to the Sun – Mercury, Venus, Earth and Mars – are all small, dense and rocky. Except for Earth, not one of them could support life as we know it. Spacecrafts have landed on Venus and Mars but they have found no evidence of life.

Mercury has no air, and is very hot on the side facing the Sun and very cold on the other side. It is covered with craters like those on the Moon.

Venus is about the same size as the Earth, but conditions on its surface are very different. It has an atmosphere of carbon dioxide, a gas which cannot support life.

There is a thick blanket of clouds around Venus, but they are not made of water vapor like our clouds. Instead, they are made of sulphuric acid, a dangerous chemical which dissolves many materials, even the metal of spaceships!

The clouds trap the Sun's heat, so that Venus is nearly as hot as Mercury, although it is further from the Sun. The surface is so hot that lead would flow in rivers!

Mars is a lot smaller than the Earth. It has a very thin atmosphere of carbon dioxide, and its surface is a sandy desert with some dead volcanoes and enormous canyons.

Even in the warmest places, the temperature hardly rises above the freezing point of water, and in fact there is no water on Mars.

There are white caps at the North and South poles, but they are probably solid carbon dioxide, not ice.

Mars has two moons circling around it, but they are much smaller than our Moon, being no more than huge pieces of rock several kilometers (miles) across.

J

THE OUTER PLANETS

Jupiter, Saturn, Uranus and **Neptune** are giant planets. About 1300 Earths could fit into the space occupied by Jupiter, the largest planet.

These giants are all extremely cold, and made of light gases. (Saturn is light enough to float in water!) They have thick, cloudy atmospheres, and may have a small solid core.

Saturn is a beautiful sight through a telescope because of its system of bright rings, made up of particles of dust and frozen gas.

Astronomers have recently discovered similar rings around Jupiter and Uranus. The rings of Jupiter were discovered in pictures taken by the Voyager spacecraft in 1979, which also showed up several new moons.

Each of these planets has a number of moons, and there may be others yet to be found.

The planet Jupiter, photographed from a Voyager spacecraft.

Pluto, the furthest planet, is an oddity. It is small and rocky. The orbits of the other planets are all nearly circular and lie almost in a flat plane, but Pluto's orbit is oval in shape and is tilted above and below the plane of the other planets. When Pluto is closest to the Sun it passes inside Neptune's orbit. It may be that Pluto is not a true planet but one of Neptune's moons which has somehow escaped.

Asteroids, comets and meteors

The **asteroids** are a belt of small bodies which circle the Sun in the large gap between Mars and Jupiter. The biggest, Ceres, is only 1000km (600 miles) across. They may be the building-blocks of a planet which never formed, due to the pull of their giant neighbor, Jupiter.

Comets are small balls of frozen gas and dust, only a few kilometers (miles) across. They move around the Sun in very oval orbits and, when they are near the Sun, the heat vaporizes some of the gas, sending a stream of gas and dust out from the comet in a tail which always points away from the Sun. They are close to the Sun for only a short time, as most of the orbit is far out among the furthest planets. The best known is Halley's comet, which returns every 76 years.

Meteors can sometimes be seen on a dark night as a sudden streak of light across the sky. A tiny piece of rock has hurtled into our atmosphere from space, and burned up as the friction of the air made it very hot. Most meteors burn up before reaching the ground, but occasionally one is large enough to hit the surface and leave a crater. The most famous is the Arizona Meteor Crater, USA, which is 1265m (4100ft) across and 175m (570ft) deep.

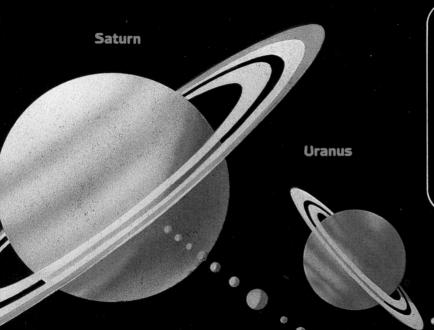

Saturn

Uranus

Neptune

Pluto

WATCH OUT FOR METEORS!

There is a chance of seeing a few meteors on any dark, clear night. However, at certain times of year the Earth passes through a comet's orbit and several meteors can be seen each hour. If you live north of the Equator, a week or so either side of August 12th, or December 10th – 16th, are good times to watch. Those living south of the Equator should watch between about July 23rd and August 6th.

THE GALAXY – FACT AND FANTASY

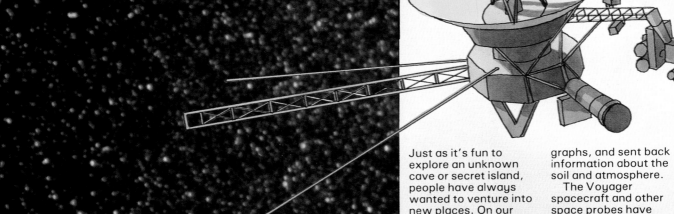

LET'S EXPLORE

Just as it's fun to explore an unknown cave or secret island, people have always wanted to venture into new places. On our own planet, people have visited islands, climbed the highest mountains, gone on expeditions to the North and South Poles and explored the depths of the sea. Now our eyes are turned outwards – can we get into space?

In 1969, American astronauts set foot on our own satellite, the Moon. More recently, the unmanned Viking spacecraft landed on Mars, took photo-graphs, and sent back information about the soil and atmosphere.

The Voyager spacecraft and other space probes have visited other planets. It was too dangerous to send astronauts on these journeys – no one knew what the spacecraft would find. Also these trips take a long time. The Voyager spacecraft is taking twelve years to reach the outer planets. Light could get there in five and a half hours, but spaceships are much slower than light! Could we ever reach the stars?

In the deep-freeze

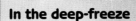

Some writers have had the idea of deep-freezing all the people on their spaceships without killing them, so that they could survive a journey of many years and not die of old age before reaching their destination. We are warm-blooded animals, and this would be very difficult, but embryos have survived freezing, so it may not be impossible.

Look into the sky on a clear night and you will see a faint hazy band of light spreading across part of the sky. This is the Milky Way. Seen through a telescope it turns out to be a thick cloud of stars. Our Sun is just one of them, a medium-sized star near one edge of the cloud. All the bright, individual stars that we can see are part of it too. It is the Milky Way Galaxy, a spiral-shaped cloud of 180 billion stars.

The stars are much further away than the planets. They are so distant that measurements in miles or kilometers become meaningless. Instead, we use the time their light takes to reach us to give us an idea of the distance. Light has the fastest speed in the Universe, 300,000km (186,000 miles) every second.

Light from the planet Pluto takes five and a half hours to reach us. Light from our nearest star, a small red one called Proxima Centauri, takes over four years to arrive. And light from the opposite edge of the galaxy takes 100,000 years! Many of the other stars in the galaxy may have solar systems around them, but they are too far away to see.

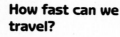

Stories about space

We have all seen films or read books about monsters on other planets, time-travel, or exciting battles in outer space. Although they may sound scientific and convincing, these stories are no more real than those about giants or fairies.

Fifty years ago people wrote books about monsters attacking us from Mars. They are good stories, but no one would write them today, because we know there is no life on Mars.

Today's writers must set their adventures further afield – and think of some way around the problems of time and distance. The best science fiction stories are often written by scientists who know a lot about space and just add one or two inventions of their own. That way it sounds as if it really could happen!

How fast can we travel?

The speed of light really is the fastest speed in the Universe. Spaceships cannot 'jump' from one sector of the galaxy to another. If light takes 100,000 years to cross the galaxy, it would take us far longer. It is difficult even to hold a conversation with Proxima Centauri, our nearest star. Our message would take four years to get there and we would have to wait another four years for a reply.

When objects begin to accelerate towards the speed of light, they get heavier, until they are so colossal that they cannot go any faster! This sounds incredible, but it has been proved to be true for electrons, very light particles which do sometimes travel extremely fast.

Time as well as mass would get distorted in a very fast spaceship.

The hours measured on the ship would be different from the hours back on Earth. You might arrive back to find that many more years had passed on Earth than you had spent on the journey, and all your friends were old and grey! Like the distortion of mass, this strange effect has been tested and found to be true. It sounds like time-travel, but there is no way we can go **backwards** in time.

Is anybody there?

The balance of conditions for life on Earth is a very delicate one. We need water, air and just the right temperature. None of the other planets of our own solar system could sustain life, and further afield is too far to see. Scientists think that because there are so many millions of stars, it is quite likely that some of them will have planets with the

right conditions. But where are they? And how far away? Radio messages are beamed out from the Earth from time to time in the hope of reaching them, but so far no one has ever replied.

Quasars and giant stars

Space stories are fun. But what is really there is just as amazing as the things we imagine. In our galaxy there are giant stars, double and triple stars, and possibly even black holes. Outside the galaxy are regions without stars – then more galaxies, quasars, and dust clouds. The farthest known galaxies are 10 billion light-years away. If the light set out from them 10 billion years ago, it's quite possible that the stars giving out the light have now died, and we are looking at what the Universe was like before there was life on Planet Earth.

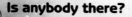

Preparing for the journey

If we were to set out into space, we would need to prepare for a very long journey. We should have to provide our own heat, light, air and water, and grow our own food on the way. We should need to produce our own fuel, and our clothes, and make repairs to the ship. On the journey, we should marry, have children, and die. And perhaps our distant descendants would find a suitable planet to land on! On the other hand, they might regard the ship as home and stay there. It would be a complete world.

Just as our sun is only one of many millions of suns which make up the Milky Way, so the Milky Way itself is only one of the millions of galaxies which make up the universe in which we live.

The galaxies are separated from each other by vast areas of more or less empty space. Most are so far apart that it takes light millions of years to travel between them.

Galaxies are not spread out evenly through space, but grouped together in clusters. Some clusters contain only a few galaxies, others many hundreds. The Milky Way is one member of our Local Cluster, which contains about 30 galaxies. Three of these can be seen with the naked eye.

People living south of the equator can see the two Magellanic Clouds. They are quite small galaxies, less than a quarter the size of the Milky Way, and very close to us in space terms – their light takes about 180,000 years to reach us.

On a clear, dark, September or October night those living north of the equator can just see the Andromeda Nebula. It appears as a faint smudge of light quite high in the southeastern sky a little above and to the east of a group of four fairly bright stars that form a large square, called the Square of Pegasus. It is the most distant object that the eye can see. Its light takes about two million years to reach us. It is a large spiral-shaped galaxy nearly twice the size of the Milky Way. If you can, look at it using binoculars or a small telescope.

The clusters of galaxies outside of our Local Cluster all seem to be racing away from us, and from each other. This means that we are living in an expanding universe. One way of illustrating this is to paint a number of black dots on a balloon and then blow it up. As it expands, each dot gets further and further away from those next to it.

A Big Bang and some Big Questions

Astronomers believe that this expansion of the universe is a result of it having begun with a 'big bang.' According to this theory there was once a time, about 15 billion years ago, when all the matter and energy in the universe came into being as a very small, very hot, ball. This exploded and, as the pieces flew apart, they cooled down. First they formed subatomic particles, then atoms, then clouds of gases, and finally galaxies.

This theory says that the universe as we know it did have a beginning, but it says nothing about the origin of the energy and matter out of which it is made.

In fact scientists cannot answer such questions as, 'Why did the Big Bang happen?' and 'Why is there matter and energy, and so a universe, at all?' They can only study the matter and energy that do exist and suggest how it might have come to form the universe that we know.

Many people, including scientists, are convinced that there must be a God who created energy and matter and formed the universe out of it. The 'Big Bang' theory may tell us how God caused the matter to become organized into a universe.

Left to itself, will the universe go on expanding forever?

Scientists cannot yet answer that question. It depends on the amount of matter in the universe. If it is less than a certain amount the answer would be 'Yes.' If there is more matter than this the attraction of gravity between the galaxies will cause the expansion to slow down and stop. The universe will then start to contract and will end up as it began, as a fiery ball of matter – but that would be in billions of years' time.

Galaxies can differ greatly in size, but they fall into one of four groups according to their shape.
● Ordinary spiral galaxies have a bright center around which are wrapped spiral arms. The Milky Way has this shape.
● Barred spirals have a

Scientists learn more about our universe by watching the skies through giant telescopes. These are at Kitt Peak National Observatory, Arizona, USA.

THE DOPPLER EFFECT

The Doppler Effect, named after the Austrian scientist who first explained it, is used to measure the speed at which the galaxies are moving.

The effect was originally noticed with sound waves. Movement causes the sound waves in front of a moving object to become bunched up, and the ones following it to be spaced out. As a result, the sound in front of the object has a higher note than the sound behind it. This is why as a jet plane approaches and then passes overhead, the sound changes from a high whine to a low roar. It is why the note of a siren on a police car changes as it passes you.

The same kind of effect is true for light waves. The bunching up of the light waves in front of a galaxy that is approaching us makes it look bluer than it would be if it were not moving. The spacing out of the light waves from one that is going away from us makes it look redder. In fact all the distant galaxies have a 'red-shift,' showing that they are going away from us. The amount of the red-shift is a measure of the speed at which they are moving.

QUASARS AND BLACK HOLES

Quasars were discovered in 1960 but are still a puzzle to astronomers. They are a fraction the size of galaxies, yet hundreds of times brighter. Some of them have very large red-shifts and are the most distant object that we can see, their light taking more than 10 billion years to reach us.

One theory is that they are the centers of galaxies in which there is a massive black hole. The very hot gases circling around the black hole make the quasar very bright.

Black holes are the result of a process called gravitational collapse. When a very large star gets old and begins to burn out it starts to collapse under its own gravity. The atoms of the star get squeezed closer and closer together and get hotter and hotter. Eventually there is a big explosion in which the outer part of the star is blown away, leaving behind it a very odd object — an infinitely small and infinitely dense 'black hole' whose gravitational pull is so strong that nothing that comes near it can escape. Everything is sucked in, even light.

THE SHAPE OF GALAXIES

bright center, crossed by a straight bar, from the ends of which come spiral shaped arms.
● Elliptical galaxies have an oval shape without arms.
● Irregular galaxies have no clear shape. The Magellanic Clouds are in this group.

A spiral galaxy.

ATOMS: BUILDING BLOCKS OF THE UNIVERSE

The microscope is a wonderful instrument to make small things look bigger. If you had the most powerful microscope in the world, you would discover that ordinary things around us are as interesting and amazing as the galaxies!

Suppose you set the microscope to look at things one billion times smaller than you. Tiny insects would seem large and ferocious, and you could watch a mosquito uncurl his proboscis to bite someone. You could look at the helicopter propeller on a dandelion seed, or the ice crystals in a snowflake. Some

Through the microscope tiny creatures like this pond skater can look very fierce.

creatures that small are light enough to walk about on the surface of water. You could watch one skating about on a pond, or catching an unwary pond-creature for his dinner.

If you set your microscope to look at things a hundred thousand times smaller than you, the world would look very different. The living creatures of that size are much simpler, sometimes just a few cells. A drop of pond water contains hundreds of them. A drop of blood might contain an influenza virus, and an antibody attacking it to make the person better. You could also see strange things that are not alive, like the huge, twisted molecules that make up a plastic bag.

If you tried to set your microscope to look at things one billion times smaller than you, the microscope would not work! No microscope using light can show us things as small as that. You would just see a blur. Yet that is the size of an atom, one of the building blocks of the universe! How do scientists know about atoms when they can't even see them?

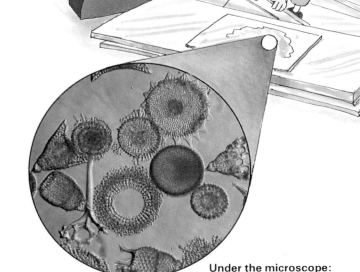

Under the microscope: protozoa.

A GIANT DETECTIVE STORY

Finding out about the atom has been like a giant detective story, with many people discovering clues. Some clues are quite easy to find if you look and think.

CLUE 1. Look at a salt crystal. It is always a cube, however big or small. This suggests that atoms in salt are arranged in a cubic pattern. Other materials also have their own special shape.

CLUE 2. Stand on the floor. You don't fall through! The atoms in the floor must hold together very firmly to support your weight.

Some clues can be found by quite simple experiments, but some modern experiments have very complicated equipment. In many experiments scientists bombard a material with tiny particles and

watch what happens. Do the particles bounce off the atoms, stick on, or break the atoms up? They have found out a lot, and have even made atoms that do not exist in nature! Scientists are now pretty sure that they are right about atoms . . . but there are still fresh clues to follow!

What are atoms?

If you cut up a piece of copper into smaller and smaller pieces, an atom is the smallest piece possible which is still copper. There are 90 sorts of atoms on earth which can occur naturally. Some, such as copper, silver and tin, are metals. Some, like the oxygen we breathe in the air, are gases.

Sometimes different types of atoms join together into groups and make a molecule which behaves quite differently from the atoms in it. Water, a liquid, is made up of hydrogen and oxygen, both gases. Salt is made of sodium, a metal, and chlorine, a gas.

Bigger molecules, such as plastics or sugar, are made of

many different atoms and are very complicated.

Living cells are made of big molecules, and plants and animals are made of living cells. This is how everything around us is built up.

Inside the atom . . .

hydrogen atom

nucleus

electron

helium atom

electron proton neutron

lithium atom

. . . we find a new world again! Each atom is like a miniature solar system, with a heavy nucleus in the middle, and tiny particles called electrons spinning around it, like planets around the sun.

The atoms are mostly empty space, and the nucleus is unbelievably small. If you imagine a large hall with a spoonful of sugar in the center (representing the nucleus) and flies buzzing around it near the walls (representing the electrons), the scale would be about right.

All atoms are like this, but different types have different numbers of electrons and particles in the nucleus. The diagram shows what we think some of them are like – but remember they are too small to see. All this has been discovered by piecing together clues from different experiments.

A COLLECTION TO MAKE

Try to make a list of words that could describe materials – hard, springy, shiny, clear, for example. Then try to find a piece of something to go with each word. See if you can find out what the materials are used for, and why. Look at them through a magnifying glass if you have one.

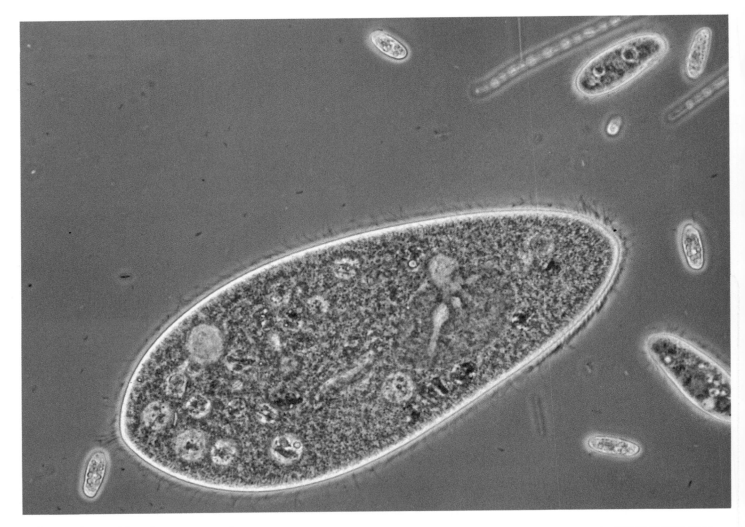

When science first began, people thought that living and non-living objects were quite different. For example, a piece of copper is not alive, and an ant is alive. However, we know now that the ant is made of chemicals such as carbon, hydrogen and oxygen.

Carbon on its own (a piece of coal) and the oxygen in the air are certainly not alive, yet it seems that when the right chemicals are combined in the right complicated pattern, something entirely new can happen – life.

But the life all around us has not come from scientists arranging chemicals. It has come from creatures reproducing, making baby creatures like the parents. Scientists know a lot about how living things work, but they have not yet made living things themselves.

HOW CAN WE TELL SOMETHING IS ALIVE?

All living things have certain properties in common.

● They all feed, taking in the chemicals they need and getting rid of the waste products.

● They all react to what is going on around them. (For instance, you 'jump' when you hurt yourself; a plant bends towards the light.)

● They grow.

● They reproduce themselves.

Sunflowers turn to face the sun: like all living things they react to what goes on around them.

● They move, though plants move much less than animals.

● They 'respire,' which is related to breathing, using oxygen and giving out carbon dioxide. Even seeds do this, and growing seeds can suffocate if they are deprived of oxygen for a long time.

The living cell

Because most cells are too small for us to see without a microscope, they were not discovered until after the microscope was invented. But we know that all living things are made up of cells.

Each cell has a thin, flexible skin called a membrane around it. This holds in the contents and allows some substances to enter or leave the cell,

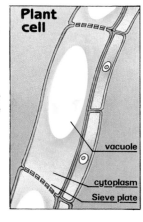

Plant cell

vacuole

cytoplasm

Sieve plate

passing through tiny gaps in the membrane and keeping the conditions inside the cell just right.

Inside is a jelly-like substance called protoplasm, which is living, and is controlled by the nucleus, the center of activity.

Under the microscope we can see the structure of a living cell.

The nucleus controls cell division, which is how the creature grows, and also the passage of chemicals into and out of the cell. The cell cannot work properly if the nucleus is taken out.

Plant cells also have a cell wall which is made by the protoplasm. It is flexible while the cell is growing, but may become tough and rigid when the cell is full size. The woody trunks

of trees are built up in this way. Plant cells usually contain cavities ('vacuoles') full of sap, which presses outwards and keeps the cells firm.

HOW LIVING THINGS GROW

All living things start off as one cell, and look fairly alike. But in the more complex animals and plants the cells divide over and over again, until there are millions of them. (Can you work out how many there would be after just ten divisions of all the cells?)

The simplest creatures, called protozoa, have just one cell, which carries out all the tasks needed to keep the protozoa alive and reproduce itself.

In larger creatures, most of the cells

Cell division

1   **2**   **4**   **8**

develop in special ways to carry out different jobs and all work together for the good of the animal or plant, like a factory with lots of workers.

A muscle cell works to move an animal's limb, but it cannot get its own food or oxygen. It relies on

other cells for those.

Some cells – for instance the nerve cells which carry messages to your brain from different parts of the body, or the sting cells on a jellyfish – have very strange shapes.

Cells as complicated as these cannot divide and form new cells.

That is why complex creatures cannot grow a new arm or leg if one is cut off in an accident. Worms and starfish have simpler cells and can recover by growing a new part.

In plants, some cells are long and cylindrical. They are green and soft when

young, but when old they produce a woody wall and the contents die, leaving a tube. The layers at the top and bottom break down, and tubes arranged on top of each other carry water from the roots to the tops of tall trees, just like pipes.

Your own special code

The nucleus of each cell of your body contains a complicated arrangement of atoms which is the same for all the cells of your body. It is different from anybody else's arrangement.

Before you were born, as the cells divided, your own special pattern was given to each new cell, whatever its job was going to be. Somehow

the right number of cells became muscle cells, nerve cells, red blood cells, bone cells, and so on, until you were a complete person.

As you get older some of your cells die and are replaced. By the time you are grown up hardly any of the cells which were there when you were a baby are left. And yet the new cells still carry

your own special code. You are still you!

This amazing story is true for every living organism. It is not surprising that, although scientists have been able to watch what happens, they have not yet been able to copy it. We can see in the growth of even the simplest creature something of the Creator's marvelous design.

LIKE PARENT, LIKE CHILD

'Who does she look like?'
'He's got his dad's nose!'
'Isn't she like her mother?'
These are the sorts of things people say when they see a new baby.

Children are like their parents in some ways, but usually they have a mixture of characteristics from both parents, not just one.

Jane may have dark hair and brown eyes like her mother, but be tall like her father.

John may be good at tennis like his mother and musical like his father.

In some ways we may seem different from both parents – maybe we take after a grandparent.

It isn't only people who inherit a mixture of their parents' qualities. It is true for plants, insects and other living creatures as well. It was part of God's wonderful plan to make a world full of variety and interest. How boring it would be if every child was exactly like one of his or her parents!

How does this likeness work?

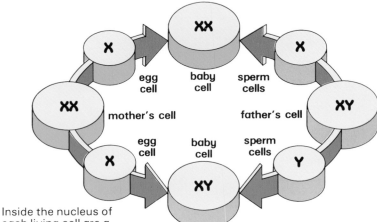

Inside the nucleus of each living cell are a number of long, threadlike molecules called **chromosomes**. They contain a special chemical with such a complicated name that it is simply called **DNA**.

The chromosomes normally exist as pairs, and the number of pairs in each nucleus is different for different kinds of creatures. Human beings have 24 pairs, mice have 40 pairs, and onions 8 pairs.

Each chromosome is made of hundreds of tiny sections called **genes**. The color of our hair, our height or musical ability, is controlled by a separate gene or group of genes. The precise combination of genes is different for every human being. No two people in the whole world, except for identical twins, are exactly alike.

For most creatures, a baby begins to form when an egg-cell from the mother combines with a sperm-cell from the father. Each of these cells contains only half the normal number of chromosomes in its nucleus – one from each pair in the parents' cells. When they combine, the new baby-cell has just the right number of chromosomes, half

from the father and half from the mother. That is why you are like your mother in some ways but your father in others. You are a special mixture of them both.

It is the sperm-cell from the father that decides whether the new baby will be a boy or girl. One particular chromosome can be either what is called an X or a Y chromosome. Girls have a pair of X chromosomes and boys have one X and one Y chromosome.

This means that when the chromosome pairs split to form egg-cells and sperm-cells, *all* the egg-cells will have X chromosomes, but half the sperm-cells will have X and half Y. As a result, when the egg- and sperm-cells combine, half the baby-cells will have a pair of X chromosomes, and will develop into little girls. Half will have an XY pair and will become boys. That is why about half the babies born are girls and half are boys.

Mutations

Ordinarily genes pass from parent to child unchanged. However, very occasionally a change occurs in the gene itself. This change is called a mutation. We do not know the causes of all mutations, though some are due to X-rays, radiation from radioactive materials, or certain chemicals.

Mutations can be beneficial to the child, but the vast majority have harmful results. This is why great care is taken to protect people from harmful radiation or chemicals.

What about twins?

Sometimes two egg-cells are fertilized separately in the mother's body, and two babies grow side by side. They will be non-identical twins, and will be no more alike or different than other brothers or sisters in the family. Sometimes, however, a baby cell divides into two after it has been fertilized, and each half becomes a separate baby. These babies are identical, since they both have the same genes. Identical twins are always either both boys or both girls.

A DNA strand. The way the components of the DNA molecule, shown here in different colors, are arranged is what determines your special genetic code.

BREEDING SPECIAL PLANTS AND ANIMALS

Because we have learned how characteristics are passed from parents to children, farmers have been able to develop better crop plants and farm animals.

For example, sometimes a few plants out of a whole field grow better than the rest, perhaps because they are more resistant than the others to insect attack. The seeds from these plants are carefully collected and used to produce more insect-resistant plants, which produce more seeds, and so on — until there are enough seeds for everyone to buy.

'Selective breeding, as this process is called, can be a real help. It means that more food can be produced from the same area of land. We can also reduce the use of chemicals to kill pests. The result is cheaper food, and not so many possibly harmful chemicals spread around the countryside.

Cattle farmers also use cross-breeding, for example mating a very large, sturdy bull with a cow that produces lots of milk. In this way the calves combine the best qualities of both animals.

SOMETHING TO DO

Make a list of the characteristics of members of your family — color of eyes and hair, whether hair is straight or curly, height and build (compared with others of the same age), interests, abilities, and so on.

Extend this as far back as you can by asking your grandparents about their parents.

Then see if you can trace the lines of inheritance through the generations.

OUR FRIENDLY EARTH

On our Earth, a great many unlikely things happen to make the planet suitable for life. If just one thing was wrong, life could not exist.

WONDERFUL WATER

It is very important for life that water starts to freeze from the top.

Scientists agree that the first living things lived in water. Many simple creatures live in water, and even complicated land animals have water inside them.

Our bodies contain a lot of water, and the chemicals which move around inside us could not do their work without water to carry them. We cannot live for long without water, though people have survived without food for many days.

There is water all over the Earth, and yet it is a very strange liquid. Many scientists have studied it, but it is still not fully understood. It has special properties which enable it to support life, and we know of no other liquid which could take its place.

Water stores heat

If you were to heat up 1kg (2.2 pounds) of copper and 1kg of water for the same length of time, you would find that when the copper was very hot, the water was hardly warm. It takes a great deal of heat to warm up water! The Sun beats down on our oceans, but they don't get very hot. They store the heat, and then at night they give it out and help to keep the Earth warm. The creatures in and around the oceans are protected from too much heat or cold.

Water freezes upside down

Nearly every liquid we know starts to freeze at the bottom, but it is very important to us that water starts to freeze at the top. In winter, many lakes and ponds freeze over and the little creatures beneath are safe from the wintry weather. If water solidified at the bottom first, they would be entombed in ice. Fewer creatures would survive, and the history of life would have been very different.

EXPERIMENT

Try tipping some melted wax or cooking fat into one cup, and water into another. (Melted wax or fat can get very hot, so ask a grown-up first.) Put the water where it will freeze. After a few minutes take another look. The wax or fat starts to solidify at the bottom, and at the edges which cool first. You will need to wait much longer for the water! When it starts to freeze, the ice will be on top.

JUST RIGHT

Our Earth is just the right distance from the Sun.

It is big enough to hold a life-giving atmosphere.

It is not too hot, nor too cold.

There is plenty of water — that strange liquid which seems the only one able to support life.

Our atmosphere shields us from many harmful things.

In comparison, the other planets we know about are unbelievably hostile. They are as hot as liquid metal, or cold enough to solidify gases. Their atmospheres, if they have them, are mostly highly poisonous. There is hardly any oxygen, and no liquid water.

Many people believe it is no accident that all these factors combine to make Earth such a friendly place. God planned it that way, because he was making a home for the living creatures in his creation, and for people who might be his friends.

A BLANKET OF AIR

Nearly all living things need oxygen to breathe. Our atmosphere is one-fifth oxygen, and the other gases do not hurt us as we breathe them in and out. To keep the oxygen near the Earth, the pull of gravity must be just the right strength.

Oxygen molecules in the air around us travel at about 0.5 kilometers per second. Scientists know that space rockets must go at 11 kilometers per second if they are to escape completely from the Earth's pull. So the oxygen molecules are too slow, and cannot escape.

The Moon is smaller, and the pull of gravity there is less, so all the gases have gone from the Moon. You could not breathe there without a spacesuit. Mercury is small too, and much hotter, as it is so near the Sun. The gases on Mercury have been speeded up by the heat and they have all gone too.

Our Earth is continually bombarded by meteorites (which are like rocks of varying size), but most of them burn up in the atmosphere and never reach the ground. Because the moon has no protective atmosphere its surface is cracked and scarred. When the Sun shines, it gets very hot, and when it is in darkness, incredibly cold. The heat and cold make the ground crack and crumble. Our atmosphere keeps the ground cooler by day and warmer by night. There is no water on the Moon. It could not stay there without an atmosphere pressing down on it. The water molecules would all fly off into space.

On the Moon, human beings cannot breathe without space suits.

A MAGNETIC SHIELD

A magnetic compass is a great help to sailors and travelers. It works because the world is a giant magnet and attracts the needle towards the North Pole. The magnetism has another, less well-known result.

At the very top of the atmosphere are many electrically charged particles – little pieces of atoms, held there by the Earth's magnetism. They act like a filter reducing cosmic rays from space and stopping some of the Sun's radiation from reaching us. The Sun produces many different kinds of radiation, and not all of them are good for us! The charged particles keep the harmful o..es out.

HOW DID LIFE ON EARTH BEGIN?

How did life begin on planet Earth?

One of the oldest known creation stories is the one found at the beginning of the Bible. It is the basis of Jewish and Christian beliefs about creation and is respected by Muslims, who also believe in a Creator God. In it we read that God said, 'Let the earth produce all kinds of plants – and the earth produced plants.' And so it was with all the other forms of life.

Scientists have tried to see whether they can discover how the earth might have produced life.

Life as we know it depends on the existence of certain vital chemicals. If they were not there, it could not have happened.

The DNA in the nucleus of the living cell is made of a type of sugar and chemicals called nucleic acids. Most of the chemical processes which go on in living cells are controlled by proteins, which are large molecules made up of simpler molecules called amino acids. The cell walls contain sugars and fats.

All these important chemicals are made of atoms, which were there early in the life of planet Earth. But how did they come together into the right pattern for life to start? Could this have happened in a way we can understand?

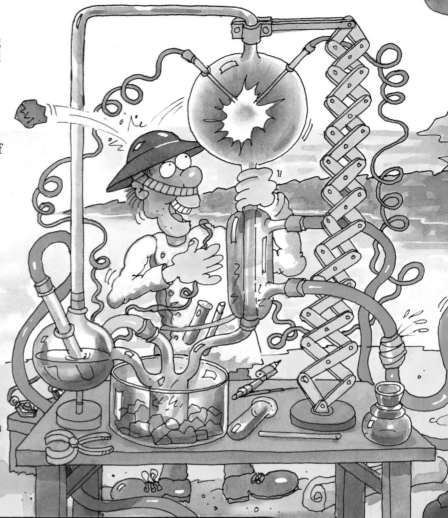

EXPERIMENTS

Some interesting experiments have been carried out to test ideas about how the molecules needed for life could have been produced. The scientists imagined what the Earth might have been like in those early days and tried to copy what could have happened.

In one experiment, the scientists imagined that the atmosphere of the Earth might have contained gases different from those in the present atmosphere. The gases could have been those which are on the outer planets today, including methane and ammonia.

The scientists mixed these gases together and let them flow through a special tube, where an enormous electric spark was produced. Then they cooled the gases down and looked at the chemicals they had made.

Some of them were amino acids, and there were also other simple chemicals which could be important for life. The scientists thought that these chemicals could have been produced on the Earth by lightning.

In another experiment, a mixture of dry amino acids was heated for several hours at a temperature well above that of boiling water. Then it was treated with hot water. The scientists found protein-like molecules dissolved in the water. They thought that

something similar might have happened on the Earth early-on, where the rocks were very hot due to volcanoes, and were then washed by rain.

Following these experiments some scientists have talked about the appearance early on the Earth of an 'organic soup' – a mixture of chemicals important for life, dissolved in pools of water or the first seas. Here, they argue, life could have started. But . . .

LIFE FROM OUTER SPACE?

A few scientists think that life could not have started on Earth because the problems are too great. They think life must have come from Outer Space – not in flying saucers or space-ships, but carried by meteorites.

It is a fact that some simple chemicals needed for life do exist in gas clouds in space, and some have been found inside the bigger meteorites. Perhaps some very simple form of life, similar to a virus, may have been formed in the gas clouds of Space, and carried to Earth on a meteorite.

Most scientists think this is very unlikely. Meteorites get very hot and often burn up when they pass through the atmosphere. It is hard to believe that even a virus, which is quite delicate, could survive great heat. Also, a type of life adapted to Outer Space would probably not survive in the different conditions on Earth.

PLAN OR ACCIDENT?

It is sometimes suggested that, given enough time, life was bound to arise by accident. The important chemicals would eventually be formed and join together in the right way. However, calculations of the chance of this happening, using modern computers, show that it is highly unlikely. The Earth would need to be far, far older than it is to give even a remote possibility of its happening.

In the Bible we are told that life on Earth is not an accident. God planned it. He created our friendly Earth so that life could exist on it. And he brought life into being, so that there would be people he could love and care for – people who could know and love him, and each other.

So far scientists have not been able to think of a way life could have started, though one day they may do so. Even if they do, it will not contradict the Bible's claim that God brought life into being on the Earth. It would only make clear the method God used. For if God is the Creator, he created the atoms and scientific laws that would make it possible. We hope that one day we will know *how* it happened. If we do, the statement that God said, 'Let the Earth produce life' – and the Earth produced life, will still be true.

SOME PROBLEMS

There are some problems with this suggestion, as other scientists have pointed out.

First of all, it is now believed that the first atmosphere after the Earth cooled down came from gases produced by volcanoes. These included water vapor, nitrogen and carbon dioxide. Sunlight shining on the water vapor would have produced oxygen. So the atmosphere would soon have become quite like our present atmosphere, which does not contain the right molecules for making the chemicals needed for life. No one can think of a way life could have started in our present atmosphere.

Then, even if the simple chemicals needed for life were somehow produced in pools of water, how could they have joined together – into such a complicated molecule as DNA? So far nobody has made a convincing suggestion.

Another problem is that the simple chemicals needed for life combine quite easily with other common chemicals to make substances which cannot be used for life – and so they would soon have been used up.

Perhaps most important of all, there is a big difference between a mixture of complicated molecules, and a well-organized cell. How did this organization start? So far, no one knows!

FOSSILS

One day in 1810 Mary Anning, eleven years old, was playing beneath the cliffs by the sea at Lyme Regis in southern England. She noticed what looked like some bones in the cliff-face. In fact she had found the first complete fossil skeleton of an ichthyosaur, a fish-like dinosaur. As a result she became one of the first great fossil hunters.

Long before her time, however, people had come across fossilized bones, shells, and plants, and had puzzled over them, wondering how they came to be there in the rocks.

Only a few of the many millions of plants and animals that die form fossils. Most decay, or are eaten by scavenging animals.

A fossil will form only when an animal dies in a place where it will soon be covered by sand or mud, and so be protected from scavengers. This is most likely to happen on the bottom of the sea or a lake, or in the mud of a river estuary.

The flesh of the body will usually decay before the remains are covered by the mud and silt, which then covers the skeleton.

As mud piles up over the years the weight of it squashes the mud around the skeleton and eventually the pressure turns it into rock. During this period the water seeping through the mud gradually dissolves away the bones, but the gaps are usually filled up by the minerals carried in the water. As a result the bone is turned to stone – 'petrified.' So the fossils which we find today are stone copies of the original bones or shells. They come to light when the movements of the Earth's crust raise the rocks containing them above the sea. Sun, wind and rain then weather them, wearing them down until we can see the fossils.

Animal footprints left in wet mud can also be preserved when the mud is dried and baked hard by the sun before it is covered by a fresh layer of mud. These fossilized footprints tell us a lot about the size of the animals and how they walked.

FOSSILIZED HISTORY

Here is a fossilized fern.

About six million different kinds of plants and animals are known only from their fossil remains. This is more than the number alive on Earth today.

As people studied fossils and the rocks in which they are found, it became clear that certain types of fossil animals and plants always occur together. This suggests that these plants and animals were all alive at the same time at a particular period in the Earth's history, and then died out and were replaced by other types.

In some places several different types of fossil-bearing rocks occur on top of each other. Here it is reasonable to believe that the top layers of rock have formed in more recent times than those lower down. In this case we can see the order in which the different types of plants and animals came and went in the history of the Earth.

The oldest fossil-bearing rocks contain only fossils of the

FREAK FOSSILS

During the last Ice Age animals sometimes fell into snow-filled gullies and died. More snow piled on top of them and turned into ice. They have remained in these natural refrigerators for thousands of years without decaying. Some woolly mammoths have been found intact in Siberia and one is now on display in a museum in Leningrad in the USSR.

Near Los Angeles, USA, there are natural deposits of tar. Many thousands of years ago, when the tar was liquid, wild animals were trapped in it. Today people digging up the hardened tar have found bones of mammoths, saber-toothed tigers, bison and other animals.

The bark of some pine trees oozes a sticky resin. Insects sometimes get stuck to it and encased in it. They are preserved in perfect condition as it hardens into amber.

MAKE YOUR OWN FOSSIL

If there is a museum near you, visit it and see if there are fossils on display. The museum staff may be able to tell you of local places where fossils can be found. In any case you can make a fossil of your own.

1 Buy some plaster of paris from a hobby shop or pharmacy. Fill a container with fine sand which is just damp enough to stick together.

2 Press a shell or bone into the sand and then remove it carefully.

3 Mix the plaster with water, following the instructions which come with it, and pour it carefully into the hollow left in the sand. When it has set you will have an imitation fossil.

A fish has been fossilized in this rock.

simpler forms of sea creatures – sponges, corals, and a creature called a trilobite.

Later rocks contain fossilized shellfish, and then various kinds of primitive fish. Land plants occur along with these fish.

Then came rocks with fossils of amphibians, animals which spend much of their time in water but can also live on land, like frogs and toads today.

More recent rocks still have fossils of reptiles, egg laying animals like the crocodile and turtle. Some lived in water, others on land, and some could even fly. Dinosaur fossils occur in these rocks.

The most recent rocks contain fossils of birds and of mammals, the warm-blooded, hairy animals which give birth to live babies.

Scientists have built up their ideas of the history of life on Earth from the order in which these fossils appear in the layers of rock.

AS OLD AS THE HILLS?

Quite often as you drive along an old road, or look at the face of a cliff or a quarry, you can see different layers of rock, one on top of another. It seems that the layers were formed one after another so that the oldest is at the bottom and the most recent at the top. In this way we can discover the age of one layer of rock in relation to the others.

Of course, it is not always as simple as that. The movements of the Earth's crust that produce earthquakes and push up the mountain ranges shift and bend the rocks, so that the layers are often jumbled up, and sometimes even turned upside down! Also wind and rain, glaciers and rivers, can wear away layers of rocks that once existed, so that there are gaps in the record which we do not know about. However, by a careful study of the rock layers over a large area, geologists – the scientists who study rocks – can usually sort out the jumble and discover the original order in which the rocks were formed.

Weathering has laid bare these layers of rock in Bryce Canyon National Park, Utah, USA.

How old is this rock?

No one could really answer that question until scientists discovered radioactivity and began to understand it.

Some atoms are naturally unstable. They break down into lighter atoms, giving out radiation in the process. Each type of radioactive atom has a constant breakdown rate. After a certain time only half the original amount of material is left. This time is called the *half-life*. For uranium-238 it is 4 billion 500 million years!

This means that if we start with 1g of uranium-238, after 4 billion 500 million years only $\frac{1}{2}$g will be left; after another 4 billion 500 million

years only $\frac{1}{4}$g will be left and so on. The rest will have changed to lead-206. The half-lives of different radioactive atoms vary from millions of years to fractions of a second.

Minerals which contain radioactive atoms can be used to date rocks. If a layer of rock contains a uranium mineral it will also contain the lead produced by the decay of the uranium since that rock layer was formed. By measuring the amounts of uranium and lead

Movement in the Earth's crust pushes the rock layers into folds, as in this picture taken in the south-west of Britain.

A WATER CLOCK

You can make a water clock that illustrates the idea of half-life. You will need an empty, clear plastic bottle. Get a grown-up to help you cut the top off, to leave just the straight sides, and make a pinhole close to the bottom.

Measure the distance from the hole to the top, and make a mark half way up.

Make another mark a quarter of the way up. Fill it to the top with cold water.

Measure the time taken for the water level to drop to half-full and then to a quarter-full. The times will be about the same. However full the 'clock' is, it will always take the same time for half of the water to run out through the pin-hole.

---

present in the rock it is possible to work out its age.

There are problems in radioactive dating. For example, lead occurs in rock anyway, so not all the lead in the rock layer may have come from the uranium. However, natural lead differs slightly from that produced from uranium, and so its presence can be detected and allowed for.

A bigger problem is that lead may have been dissolved out of the rock by water seeping through it. This is harder to allow for, and if it happens it will make the age calculated for the rock less than it should be. However, there are

ways of reducing or avoiding this error, so that dates obtained from radioactive minerals are generally reliable. As well as uranium-238 other minerals can be used for dating, especially those containing rubidium-87 and potassium-40.

The age of the Earth

According to radioactive dating methods the oldest rocks on the Earth are about 4 billion 500 million years old. Similar ages have been found for meteorites and Moon rocks. Quite different methods of arriving at the Earth's age give similar answers.

Modern ideas about how stars are formed, develop, and eventually burn out suggest that our Sun is about 5 billion years old.

Astronomers think that the Earth was formed at about the same time as the Sun from the same cloud of dust and gas.

The present rate of expansion of the galaxies suggests that, if the universe began with a 'Big Bang,' it occurred some 15 billion years ago. This makes an age of 5 billion years for the Earth quite reasonable.

Long before radioactive dating was discovered some scholars suggested that the Earth was about 6,000 years old.

They arrived at this figure by adding up the ages of the people mentioned in the family trees given in the Bible.

However, they did not allow for the probability that the family trees are not complete but only mention the most important people in the family history.

These family trees go back to Adam, the first man mentioned in the Bible. The Bible describes him as tilling the soil and keeping animals. It says that the use of metal was first discovered by one of his descendants. This means that Adam must have used stone tools, suggesting that he lived in what is called the New Stone Age, about 10,000

years ago.

The biblical story of the creation of the world, the plants, fish, birds, and animals before Adam is presented in terms of a week of activity by God. Some people take this to mean actual 24-hour days. But the story uses picture language, and it can equally well be understood as presenting the story of creation in a way that people of all centuries could understand and appreciate. It tells us that God created our world in a planned and orderly way, by successive stages, until it was a home for men and women.

THE HISTORY OF LIFE

The Theory of Evolution is one attempt to describe the history of life on planet Earth, based on a number of different pieces of evidence. It is only a theory, a suggested explanation of the facts, and it is wise to remember that, in the history of science, many theories have come and gone as new facts, or new understandings of the facts, have come along.

FOSSIL REMAINS

The fossil record is probably the most important piece of evidence that the Theory of Evolution claims to explain. If modern dating methods are reliable, the order of the fossils in the rocks shows that in the course of several hundreds of millions of years the forms of life on earth have become more varied and more complex.

Life appeared first in the sea. Then plants, and later animals, spread onto the land. Some animals even took to the air.

This leads evolutionists to suggest that there has been a process of continual, but gradual, change from original, quite simple, single-celled creatures to all the many forms that exist today.

The fossils, however, do not give clear proof of this. The major groups of animals, such as reptiles and mammals, are very different from each other, and no fossils have been found of creatures that are clearly half-way between two major groups.

The same is even true for most types of animals within a major group. In fact new types of animals usually appear quite suddenly in the fossil record.

Of course, the record is very patchy, since few animals would have left fossil remains. However, the almost total absence of half-way forms is surprising. It has led some scientists to suggest that the process of change was not gradual but took place in sudden leaps. Some people see these as new creative acts by God, pictured by the 'days' in the Genesis story, but separated by long periods of time.

SIMILAR BUT DIFFERENT

humerus

radius and ulna

carpals and metacarpals

phalanges

 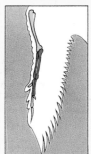 

human   crocodile   bird   bat

Outwardly the human arm, the front leg of a crocodile, a bird's wing and a bat's wing do not seem to have much in common. However, when we study their bone structure, we can see that they are all variations of the same pattern.

Evolutionists think this is best explained if the front limb of an early animal has gradually changed to produce these different forms. All these animals could then have developed from the same ancestor, their limbs being adapted to suit their different needs.

There are many such similarities between the skeletons of large groups of very varied animals. Evolutionists argue that if these animals did not come from a common ancestor but arose independently, there is no good reason for these similarities.

Of course, these similarities are not surprising either, if these creatures are the product of the mind of a Creator-God.

WINGS THAT CAN'T FLY

Some birds, such as the kiwi, have small wings that they do not use for flying.

The python has small bones resembling leg bones.

The human backbone ends in what looks like a small tail.

Things like this are called vestigial organs, that is body parts that once had an important use but no longer do so. These vestigial organs can be seen as evidence of evolutionary change.

However, many organs that were once regarded as useless vestigial ones are now known to have important uses.

The glands that produce important chemicals that control body processes were originally regarded as useless relics of an earlier stage in human development.

The appendix, also once thought to be quite useless, may in fact play a part in defending the body against disease.

Even the tail-like bones at the end of the backbone serve as an anchor point for certain muscles.

In science it is always important to admit that something which seems useless or unimportant may have a significance which we have not yet discovered or understood. We seem to know so much, yet there is still a great deal about which we are ignorant.

The kiwi has wings too small for flying. Many creatures have vestigial organs like this.

Wildlife

The animals and plants in one part of the world usually differ from those in other parts, to a greater or lesser extent.

Some places have been more or less isolated from the rest of the world by sea, or mountains, or other features, for some length of time. Evolutionists point out that, in general, the longer the period of isolation has been the greater the difference between the wildlife of that area and the wildlife elsewhere. This is taken as evidence of animals adapting to their surroundings by a process of gradual change.

A good example is Australia, which has been separated from the other continents by the sea for a long time. None of the mammals native to Australia are of the kind that dominate the rest of the world. These dominant mammals

have babies that are properly developed at birth. Australian mammals, such as the kangaroo, have pouches in which their babies can be protected for a time after birth, because the babies are not fully developed when born.

Evolutionists argue that these pouched mammals came into being before other mammals, at a time when animals could still travel between Asia and Australia. Then Australia was cut off by the sea. When the new type of mammal arose it could not get there. Instead, some pouched mammals in Australia developed into many forms similar to other mammals elsewhere that lived in similar surroundings, for example the pouched Tasmanian wolf. Without better fossil evidence than we now have, we cannot be sure that this is really how mammals developed in Australia.

THE CHEMISTRY OF LIFE

As scientists have come to understand the chemical processes of life, they have found that amazingly similar processes take place in the cells of all living creatures. For example, the way in which a sugar called glucose is turned into energy is exactly the same in bacteria and human cells, even though it is a fairly long and complicated process. Also, the way in which the details of inherited characteristics are stored in the cell nucleus and passed on, is the same in all living things. This could be evidence of development from a common ancestor, as in the case of bone structures. Many people also see it as evidence that there was a single creative mind at work, planning and producing life on Earth.

How could simple creatures change into more complicated ones?

Biologists, the scientists who study living things, point to two possible clues to the answer.

First, there is the natural variability of living things. Horses, cats, dogs, and all the other creatures come in a great variety of sizes, shapes, colors, and so on. Much of this variability is the result of characteristics controlled by genes in all the existing animals of that type. Occasionally a new characteristic appears as a result of a sudden change in one or more genes – a gene mutation. It is not clear what causes these changes, but they can be the result of radiation from radioactive minerals, or of certain chemicals.

Then there is 'natural selection.' This is the effect on the animal of the situation in which it lives. In cold areas animals with thick, hairy coats, or a thick layer of fat under their skin, will be most likely to survive and produce babies. The babies will inherit these characteristics. Eventually all the animals in that region will come to have them.

If snow is common, animals which are white or light-colored will find it easier to catch their dinner without being seen, and will be less likely to be spotted by the animals that might eat them! Once again, they are more likely to live longer and produce more babies than dark-colored animals.

There is no doubt that natural variability and natural selection do work together to produce changes in living creatures. There are some examples on this page.

The changes that have actually been observed are fairly small – the coloring of a moth, the shape of a bird's beak.

Is it reasonable to believe that, given enough time, much bigger changes could occur? Could fish produce amphibians, and so on? Many biologists think so, but some are doubtful, saying that the evidence is not strong enough.

Some believe that the idea of major change through natural selection is quite unlikely. They find it hard to imagine how a major change – from breathing through gills like fish, to breathing air through lungs as land creatures do, for example – could come about gradually. As the creature changes, it must not be at a disadvantage at any new stage of its development, or it would not survive. At present it is not clear how this could happen in such a complicated case.

Dogs

There are many different kinds, or breeds, of dogs. There is the little dachshund, the large St. Bernard, the swift greyhound, the stubborn bulldog.

The variety of dogs is the result of selective breeding. People have selected dogs with particular characteristics. By mating dogs with the same desirable characteristics, over the years they have produced different breeds of dog for different purposes.

There are tracking dogs, hunting dogs, guard dogs, sheep dogs. Some breeds have been developed simply because of a particular feature that makes them attractive – maybe their color, a silky coat, or long curly hair.

The variety of features brought out by selective breeding shows the wide range of possibilities contained within the genes of dogs. In this case, human effort has brought them out.

Evolutionists argue that it is possible to imagine selective breeding brought about simply by natural circumstances.

In wide, open grassy plains a fast-moving dog with good eyesight might be the best at catching prey – and escaping being caught. It would survive to produce babies like itself, whereas other dogs might not.

On the other hand, in heavily wooded country a good sense of smell might be of great importance for survival, since other animals would not be easy to see. The different situations would favor different kinds of dogs and so encourage their development.

THE PEPPERED MOTH

This light-colored peppered moth would be well camouflaged against a tree trunk.

The peppered moth provides a recent example of natural selection. Normally these moths are light-colored with some dark spots and lines. When the moth settles on a tree trunk it blends with the bark and is quite well camouflaged.

However, an interesting change was seen in the moths in the English Midlands and North in the second half of the last century.

At this time a great many factories were being built there. The smoke and soot which poured out of their chimneys covered the trees with grime, so that their trunks became darker. The normal peppered moth was no longer camouflaged. It stood out against the dark background, an easy prey for enemies. At this time black peppered moths appeared, which did blend with the soot-covered trees. Soon nearly all the peppered moths in these parts of England were black ones.

Today, because of anti-pollution laws and the decline of heavy industry, the trees are returning to their normal color, and the light-colored peppered moths are becoming more common.

The Galapagos finches

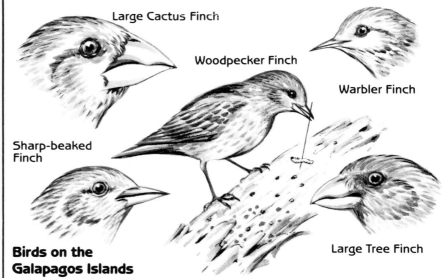

Large Cactus Finch

Woodpecker Finch

Warbler Finch

Sharp-beaked Finch

Large Tree Finch

Birds on the Galapagos Islands

The Galapagos Islands provided Charles Darwin with what he was convinced was evidence of natural selection. The Galapagos are a group of volcanic islands about 960km (600 miles) from the west coast of South America.

Darwin found that of the twenty-six types of land birds on the islands, over twenty were markedly different from similar types found in South America. On the other hand, of the eleven types of sea birds, only two were markedly different from those found on the mainland.

He believed that this was because the land birds had arrived by chance in small groups, perhaps blown there by a storm. Having settled on one of the islands they were isolated and gradually adapted to their new home by process of natural selection. Sea birds are generally more far-ranging, so there is a regular exchange between birds from the islands and birds from the coast of South America. As a result, types of sea birds specially adapted to the islands are less likely to occur.

Most of the land birds on the Galapagos Islands are varieties of finch. They differ from mainland birds in coloring, size, and shape of beak. The beaks are related to their food source. Seed eaters have strong, parrot-like beaks. Insect eaters have longer, slender beaks.

One type is a woodpecker finch. It has a straight, strong beak for wood-boring. It uses cactus spines held in its beak to dig out insects from tree bark. The finches differ on different islands, because some islands are well-wooded and favor insect eaters, while others are relatively barren.

SOMETHING TO DO

Look carefully at the dogs in your neighborhood and make a list of their different characteristics: size, color, type of coat, upright or drooping ears, type of tail . . . You can do the same for cats. Many pets are cross-breeds. In this case their babies are usually quite varied. If you know of a dog or cat that has just had puppies or kittens, ask to see them and look for differences between them and their mother, and between one another.

Wherever you live, there is a delicate balance between all living things. Some animals eat other animals. They are called carnivores, or flesh-eaters. The animals they feed on may eat plants, or perhaps insects. Many insects feed on plants, or the sap or nectar they produce, and many pollinate the plants so that they grow again the following year.

The different sorts of wildlife need each other. They must all be able to find enough food and reproduce, or they would die out.

As planet Earth developed, it went through many changes of weather and conditions, and animals and plants changed slowly to suit each situation. As we look at the fossil remains, we find that each age had its own special plants and animals, which flourished for a time, and then gave way to the next group.

The dinosaurs form one of the most exciting of these groups. No human being has ever seen a dinosaur, and many were quite unlike any animal alive today! Everything we know about them has come from detective work – studying the fossilized bones, teeth and footprints that have been found – and some ideas are still only guesses.

We can examine the bones, teeth or footprints of dinosaurs, but the softer parts rotted away and we usually have to imagine what the skin and other parts were like, using our knowledge of animals alive today. The dinosaurs seem most like today's reptiles. Reptiles have scaly or leathery skins, nearly always lay eggs, and are cold-blooded. This means they must bask in the sun to get enough body-heat to be active, and are sluggish in cool weather. But dinosaurs do not fit neatly into the reptile group.

Some batches of dinosaur eggs have been found, but so has a complete skeleton with fully-formed babies inside it, so clearly some types gave birth to live young. A fossilized imprint of a pterodactyl's body in some mud was also found – and it was hairy! This makes them more like mammals than reptiles.

There are still many unanswered questions, because the dinosaurs were so unlike anything alive today.

Diplodocus, the water giant

The diplodocus was the longest land animal that has yet been found, growing to nearly 30 meters (90ft) long. It had a huge body, legs like pillars, and a slender neck and tail. It had one nostril opening on the top of its head, and its lower bones were heavy, the upper ones light, which suggests that it spent much of its time in water.

We know too that diplodocus ate plants, because its teeth were slender and peg-like – no use at all for chewing meat, but good enough to rake the soft leaves and stems of water plants.

The brain was tiny and, like one or two other dinosaurs, diplodocus had something like a second brain near its hips, perhaps to control the tail which was such a long way from the head. Without it, a carnivore could attack the tail and run away before the head knew what had happened!

Tyrannosaurus Rex, the terrible flesh-eater

One of the most famous land dinosaurs was Tyrannosaurus Rex, or the 'tyrant lizard king.' It was nearly 16 meters (50ft) long, and everything about it tells us it was a flesh-eater (carnivore).

It had a mouthful of ferocious teeth, as long as a man's hand, vicious claws, and powerful back legs on which it ran after its prey.

Its front legs were too small even to carry food to its mouth, and its long powerful tail would have helped to balance it as it ran.

Claw marks in mud have shown us that such carnivores could swim as well as run in pursuit of peaceful plant-eaters like diplodocus.

Flying pterosaurs

The pterosaurs were some of the strangest dinosaurs. They had a huge flap of skin stretching from the body and back leg to the arm and one very long finger. This served as a wing, and pterosaurs probably glided on air currents, beating their wings occasionally to manoeuvre, as some large birds do today.

There were claws on the other short fingers, and on the hindlegs, which were possibly used for roosting upside-down like bats.

Pterosaurs came in various sizes, some quite small, though one of the largest, the pteranodon, had a 7 meter (20ft) wingspan. They may have lived on insects, or swooped low over the lakes for fish.

WHY DID THEY DIE?

The dinosaurs were successful animals. They dominated the Earth for millions of years. During that time, they changed in many ways, as they adapted to changing conditions. Then, finally, something happened that they could not adapt to and, about 65 million years ago, they all died out — land, sea and air dinosaurs disappearing at about the same time.

The reason is still a mystery.

Some people have suggested a sudden change in temperature, caused by a flare-up of the Sun, or clouds of dust in the air from volcanoes or an enormous meteorite.

Perhaps the dinosaurs were killed by disease, or deadly rays from a distant exploding star.

Perhaps the climate became too cold for them.

Somehow, the balance of life was seriously upset, and the lords of the Earth disappeared. There was room for a new beginning. The first small mammals, and the forerunners of birds and fish, survived, spread, and took over the Earth.

WHEN THE ICE CAME

The deep fjords on the west coast of Norway were carved out long ago by ice.

The Ice Ages started about 1½ million years ago. The ice did not cover the whole world, but huge ice-sheets spread from the poles and mountains, changing the surface of the planet in many ways. This happened a number of times. Each cold period lasted for thousands of years. In between were warm periods, when the ice retreated. Hot countries had wet and dry periods at the same time, so the whole world was affected. Almost all the remains of our early ancestors come from this period: this is the age of the cave men.

There are still ice sheets and glaciers in the world, so we can discover the telltale signs ice leaves behind.

A glacier is a river of ice. Glaciers are caused when snow falls on mountains in winter and the summers are not warm enough to melt it all. The snow is squashed into ice and then slides down into the valleys, usually moving about a meter each day. On the way it picks up huge boulders, scrapes them along the rocks and carves the mountainsides into strange shapes. When it meets warm air it melts and drops the boulders, sometimes in places where the surrounding rocks are quite different.

In many parts of the world where there is no ice today, we find grooves in the rocks, huge boulders stranded on rocks of a different sort, and many other signs that glaciers were once there. The beautiful fjords in Norway, New Zealand, Canada and Chile were carved by ice.

At times during the Ice Ages the ice reached as far as the River Thames in England, central Germany, and moved across the Canadian border south into the USA. In the southern hemisphere it covered New Zealand, part of Australia and the tip of South America.

Since all this ice had to come from the oceans, the level of the sea was about 100 meters (30ft) lower than it is today. The bed of the North Sea was dry, and there were land bridges linking continents and islands in various places. In fact early men and animals crossed from Russia to America on foot!

Finding out what happened

Survival or extinction?

Very little can live where the ground is covered in ice. Of course the plants and animals did not know what was happening and could not plan what to do about it.

Animals must have moved gradually away from the ice. Sometimes, by chance, they found a route that led to safety.

Babies which were born extra large, or with longer hair, would stand a better chance of survival, and live to produce more babies, so that in time the animals became large and woolly.

Remains have been found of giant sheep, oxen, baboons, lions, woolly rhinoceros, deer, and even vultures, as well as mammoths.

Cave bears, which died out early in the Ice Ages, hibernated in winter, and their bones show signs of disease. So perhaps they huddled in their caves, sleepy with cold, and died of disease and starvation.

The plants could not move, and were killed. But a few might survive on a sheltered slope facing the sun. When the ice retreated, the plants that could disperse their seeds most successfully would recolonize the area. Perhaps a bird carried a berry or seed, or the wind blew the seeds back.

The layers of soil show that each time the ice retreated, some, but not all, of the types of wildlife which were there earlier, returned.

Cave men at work

This cave painting at Altamira in Spain pictures the animals the hunters caught.

During this time, there is plenty of evidence of early human beings and their activities. As well as bones, we have the paintings they made in their caves, showing what the animals looked like and how they caught them.

There are the remains of pits they dug for trapping the giant animals, and flint clubs and spears for killing them.

There are the hearths of cooking fires, and signs of fire used in hunting or clearing woodland.

Hunters may have caused the extinction of some types of animals, such as the giant elk, and perhaps even the woolly mammoth, which survived to the very end of the Ice Ages.

WHY DID THE ICE AGES HAPPEN?

Nobody knows the real answer to that question, but there have been lots of guesses. It takes only a slight change in the weather to make a glacier shrink or grow. A drop in the average temperature of the world of only $5-8°C$ ($17-21°F$) would be enough to cause an Ice Age.

Perhaps there were variations in the heat from the center of the Earth, or the amount of radiaton from the Sun. Perhaps a giant meteorite fell and caused dust in the air, or some other factor changed the amounts of gases, so that less of the Sun's radiation reached the Earth.

Probably several things worked together to cause more snow, which reflected more of the Sun's rays, so that the Earth grew colder.

We do not know if there will be another Ice Age – perhaps we are in a warm period, and thousands of years from now the ice will come again.

THINGS TO DO

Try making an ice cube with a frozen plastic animal inside it to surprise your friends. First let a little water freeze in the bottom of the ice cube tray because, remember, water freezes at the top first. Then put in the plastic animal and a little more water to freeze it in place.

Finally fill the tray with water.

Try digging a small area of soil, so that it is completely free of all plants. Then keep a diary and see which plants get back to it first, and how.

Scientists can find out about the Ice Ages by pushing a long narrow tube deep into the earth, so that the layers of soil are kept in the right order. The oldest layers are at the bottom.

The scientists study the layers with a microscope, looking for fossilized pollen grains, beetles and other tiny creatures.

The pollen grains show which trees were growing. This gives some idea of how warm it was, since the same types of trees are alive today and will only grow at certain temperatures.

The layers show that the climate got colder and warmer again several times as the ice sheets grew and retreated.

The remains of larger animals can tell us a great deal if we study the surroundings carefully, to fit them into the right period.

In Siberia, where the ground is permanently frozen, woolly mammoths and other creatures have been found whole and perfectly preserved in the ice. The food in their stomachs shows what they lived on. The mammoths of the warm periods had much shorter hair than those of the cold ones.

Creatures such as the lion, rhinoceros and hippopotamus have been found much further north than they live today. In southern England, remains of mammoths have been found in the cold layers and remains of hippopotamuses in the warm layers.

A VERY SPECIAL CREATURE

As we look at the world around us, we marvel at the strange and beautiful creatures that still exist, or that did exist in days gone by. But surely the strangest and most wonderful creatures are ourselves! Where do we fit in? Why do we seem different from other animals?

When we are growing in our mothers' bodies, we don't look too different from a baby rabbit, or even a fish growing in an egg. We are made from the same sorts of molecules as other animals. We are mostly water, but also contain some carbon (like coal), chalk, salt, iron and small amounts of phosphorus and other things. None of these chemicals is very expensive, so if we add up the cost of our ingredients we are not worth very much. People who have gold fillings in their teeth would be worth the most!

After we are born, we still look very similar to one group of animals, the monkeys and chimpanzees. Chimpanzees are the most intelligent of animals. They can also catch influenza and other illnesses that affect us. They look so similar to us that people have thought we must be related in some distant way. But one major difference is our much larger brain.

This makes a very big difference. It means that we can think, talk and learn. Animals make noises to warn each other, or ask for food, and they can learn to solve quite difficult puzzles. We can't tell how much they can think just by looking at them, but it does not seem likely that their thinking is as complicated as ours.

We can plan things, imagine things, and we can know the difference between right and wrong. We can also pray. In every country and tribe, people look outside themselves towards a God or gods. Why do they do it?

Our larger brain makes us different from the animals. We can study the world around us – even newts in a jam jar!

People are able to plan and imagine, and to think up new challenges – like this boy on his bike.

A special purpose

In the first book of the Bible, we are told that God made human kind 'in his own image'. We are special creatures, designed to be like God in some ways. We can make plans, create things, and enjoy beauty and friendship. That is very like the Bible's picture of God. If God made us to be his helpers in looking after the Earth, as the Bible tells us, it is not surprising that people want to know him – and feel guilty when they have done something he would not like.

Christians and scientists have sometimes argued with each other because the story of the creation of Adam and Eve in the Bible seems very simple, and the evidence collected from fossils seems very complicated. The Bible talks as if God created people all at once but some man-like fossils are millions of years old. We do not have a complete set of fossils from every age, but there are fossils of ape-like creatures which some people think may have been early men.

Some Christians think that the story in Genesis is a simple, picture-like way of describing the process of evolution as the method God used to make men and women. Others think the fossils were not men at all. Most scientists think that the theory of evolution is the most likely description of the way people developed.

The most important point of the Bible story in Genesis is that God made us, however he did it, and planned that we should love and care for each other, and for the world he created. Our ability to love each other is one way in which we are like God.

THE EVOLUTIONARY VIEW

New World monkeys
Old World monkeys
apes
Australopithecus
modern / man
Neanderthal man

millions of years before the present

60 50 40 30 20 10 0

This diagram gives a picture of how scientists think the fossil ancestors of people, apes and monkeys, may have been related to one another. Since no clear 'missing links' have yet been found, this picture cannot be proved to be right. Australopithecus is the name given to some fossil creatures found in Africa. They are thought to have been man-like and died out about 1 million years ago.

Fossils of Neanderthal Man have been found in Europe, Asia and Africa. He differed from us in several ways, and was alive at the same time as the first fossils recognizable as modern man. Neanderthal Man died out about 30,000 years ago.

THE GARDEN OF EDEN

'In the beginning God created the heavens and the earth . . . God made two great lights – the greater light to govern the day and the lesser light to govern the night. He also made the stars . . . God created the great creatures of the sea . . . and every winged bird . . . God made the wild animals . . . And God saw that it was good . . .

'Then God said, "Let us make man in our image, in our likeness, and let them rule over the fish of the sea and the birds of the air, over the livestock, over all the earth, and over all the creatures that move along the ground."

'So God created man in his image, in the image of God he created him; male and female he created them . . .

'God saw all that he had made and it was very good.'
From the first book of the Bible: Genesis, chapter 1

The Genesis story says that Adam and Eve lived in a beautiful garden called the Garden of Eden. Some of the details have led scholars to think that it was in the uplands of eastern Turkey. The story also says that Adam tilled the soil and tamed the animals. Remains dug up in eastern Turkey suggest that, 10,000 years ago, the first farmers were at work there, at the start of the New Stone Age. In the Stone Age only stone tools were used, because the way to make metal tools had not yet been discovered.

Genesis suggests that Adam used stone tools, because later it tells us that one of his descendants was the first to use metal. The story of Genesis fits with what we know about the New Stone Age.

An arrangement of particles makes an atom, an arrangement of atoms makes a cell, an arrangement of cells makes a living creature. At each stage, as the pattern gets more complicated, something new and exciting happens. It is like playing with letters. A few letters make a word, more letters make a sentence, and if there are enough letters a whole new world of ideas and meaning can be built up.

We marvel as we look at some of the wildlife around us.

Think of honeybees, which make such perfect structures of wax in which to store their eggs and babies, and work together like a factory, each bee having its own special task.

Think of a flowering creeper, scrambling over walls and fences to reach the air and sunlight it needs for life, lifting up marvelously shaped flowers,

with delicate colors and stores of nectar to attract the bees, and a scent that fills the air!

People are more remarkable still.

We can do things that the animals and plants cannot do, thinking things out, designing and making new things, foreseeing problems and working out how to overcome them, sharing our ideas with one another in words, loving and caring for each other, enjoying color, music and the beauty around us. We can understand and enjoy planet Earth in a way animals cannot.

FINGERPRINT ALBUM

Everyone has a different fingerprint. You can make a fingerprint easily if you have a rubber stamp pad or printing pad, or you can make a pad from paper tissue dipped in *washable* ink.

Put your finger lightly on the pad and then on a piece of paper. It may take several tries to get a good print.

You could collect the fingerprints of your family and friends.

Science has its limits

People can reach outside themselves into realms beyond science. Scientists ask *how* something has happened, and piece the clues together until they understand it. They do not ask *why* the world was made, because they cannot take measurements to find the answer to that sort of question. But it is still a good question to ask!

People everywhere have a sense that some things are right and some are wrong. People in different countries and centuries have not always agreed exactly on everything that was thought to be good or bad, but some things are the same for everyone.

We all agree that we must tell the truth to people we love and trust.

We know that we should love and care for the very young or very old.

We share a sense of horror when we hear of people murdered, dying of starvation or of someone let down by their best friend. Where do these feelings come from? How does a collection of cells have a conscience?

Science cannot answer these questions.

In the Bible we read that we were made in the image of God, and so these parts of ourselves which we cannot fully explain show something of God's nature inside each one of us. We were made with the ability to know and love God, and in every country there are people who pray, trying to reach outside themselves to the Being with the answers. They feel sure he must be there, even though they cannot see him!

Everyone is special

In a family we are all loved, and all different. We each have our own abilities which we can use to do many things, and we each need the other members of the family. God tells us in the Bible that he is our heavenly father. Each one of us is different and special, designed to fit into his worldwide family. We all have an important part to play. He designed *you* because he wanted a person like you in the world!

All together

Some things can be done only if many people help. Exploring the sea bed to repair an oil rig is too difficult and dangerous for one person alone. Building a house needs people with many different skills. Teams of people must learn to work together, helping and trusting each other. Each person is important, even if their job is small. When the team is successful, everyone shares the joy of the achievement.

God's plan for planet Earth is that people should form one big family, working together to look after the world, the wildlife and each other, receiving instructions and help directly from him as their father and friend. It is such a big task that we must all be part of it, working together.

Working on an oil pipeline deep down in the sea requires teamwork.

In this picture, drawn by 12-year-old Craig, we see how interested he is in how this engine works.

In this poem, Andrew uses words beautifully to draw pictures in our minds.

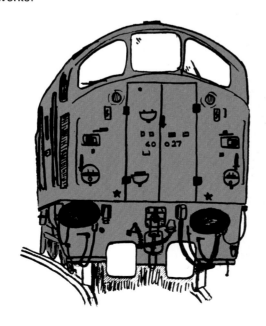

Silence

Silence is a cool breeze
  lovely in your face.
Silence is the night
  creeping over field and hill.
Silence is the moving tree
  which the wind may blow.
Silence is the creeping mouse
  after all the cheese.
Silence is the moving clouds
  gentle over the moon.
Silence is the snowflake
  dropping gently to the ground.

Andrew David Wright (9)

When we think what people can do, and the wonderful possibilities when a team of people really works together, it comes as a dreadful shock to look at planet Earth today. In many ways, it seems, the dream of what the world could be like has changed to a nightmare.

At the very beginning of the Bible, we are told that God's task for men and women was to rule over the plants and animals, taking care of them for him. Instead of that, people have thoughtlessly destroyed the woodlands, hedgerows and marshes which many animals need in order to survive.

Chemical fertilizers which produce bigger crops have been washed into the rivers by rain, poisoning countless water-creatures and the birds which live on them.

Huge tankers have washed out their tanks at sea, leaving patches of oil which have coated the beaches and caused death to sea-birds and other creatures.

Factories and cities have pumped filth and garbage into the rivers and air. Many types of wildlife are extinct, or on the list of endangered species.

The panda is only one of many animals at risk on planet Earth today.

Oil spilled in the sea means death for this penguin unless it gets help.

Fair shares for all?

We are always hearing of areas of the world where people do not have enough to eat. At the same time, in some places there is a wonderful choice of types of food which have arrived by ship from all over the world.

In some places people can visit a doctor or dentist whenever they feel like it. In others, they have to wait months for a doctor to visit their area, and may then die because they were too late receiving treatment.

The oil and coal we use to produce heat and electricity are being removed from the ground very quickly to keep all our machines running, and they cannot be replaced. In some parts of the world electricity is wasted by leaving advertising signs lit up all night. In others, children cannot go to school because they have to spend every day hunting for scarce firewood to cook the family's meals.

There is enough food in the world for everybody, but not everybody has enough. We have enough medical knowledge to cure many of the world's diseases, but they are not all cured. What has gone wrong with God's wonderful plan?

These Ethiopian children go hungry while other countries have more than they need.

Our beautiful planet is spoiled by what we throw away.

Freedom to choose

In a colony of ants or bees, the insects work together by instinct. They play their part without thinking about it, because they are not intelligent enough to think. The worker bees do not suddenly decide they would like to be queens!

But people have the power to say 'yes' or 'no.' Inside each one of us, alongside the talents and gifts to do great things, is a streak of selfishness and rebellion. Sometimes we actually enjoy spoiling something, or hurting another person. Sometimes we are too busy to care.

The Bible's explanation is that, at some time in the past, people decided they did not want God to tell them what to do. They preferred to run their own lives and plan things so that they had as comfortable a time as possible.

Just like children who do not enjoy sharing their toys, the people who have a wide choice of food do not want to make do with less so that others do not starve.

Store owners do not want to switch off their advertisements at night because fewer people would buy their goods.

Factory owners do not want to spend more money cleaning their waste products so that they do not pollute the air and the rivers. Governments sometimes pass laws to make people take more care, but laws cannot change the ideas in our minds.

We tend to work as little selfish units, all pulling in different directions, instead of playing our part as members of a worldwide family. It is not surprising that we are not looking after our complicated planet very well.

Some people have asked why God did not make us work together by instinct, like ants or bees. Then the world would have been looked after properly. The answer the Bible gives is that God wanted us to work together because we love him and each other, not because we have to! Love is not love if, like a puppet, you can't help what you do. Having the freedom to choose to love also means being free to rebel.

PROJECT – MAKE A COLLAGE

A collage is a poster made up of words cut from newspapers. Draw the shape of a large pair of eyeglasses on a big piece of paper. In one lens stick words which show what the world should be like. In the other stick words which show how ugly it is when it is spoilt. The collage will show the two sides of ourselves.

There is a dragon inside me

There is a dragon inside me,
Bewildered, puzzled and confused
Snoring all day.

There is a dragon inside me,
Fearless, brave and bold,
Spitting fire.

There is a dragon inside me,
Miserable, wretched and depressed,
Ashamed of showing himself.

There is a dragon inside me,
Clumsy, unwieldy and ungainly,
Tripping himself up.

Catherine Mary Chambers (9)

In this poem, Catherine shows us what a strange mixture of things is inside us, good, bad, hard to understand and control.

In this century scientists have come to understand the universe and the laws behind it better than ever before. They have learned to use this knowledge in new and exciting ways. Supersonic aircraft streak through the skies; home computers are as cheap as TV sets; modern buildings of new materials rise above our cities; cures have been found for many diseases. But will all this knowledge lead to a happier future? Our new knowledge can be used either for good or for bad purposes. The aircraft can be armed with the latest weapons; cruel governments can use computers to store information about all their citizens; the knowledge about diseases can be used to plan germ warfare.

The problem is that men and women, girls and boys, all too often do what is wrong rather than what is right. We find it easier to control some of the powers of nature than to control ourselves and our selfishness. There is a power of evil in the world that sometimes is too strong for us to overcome, and we give in to it.

But the power of evil is not too strong for God. He has shown us this in Jesus Christ. In Jesus, God became a man and lived a life of love and goodness. At every point of his life he overcame evil. When wicked people put him to death on a cross like a criminal, he rose from the dead and came back to life, showing that the power of God is greater than all the evil in the world. He promised that the same power of God can change us, if we will ask God to give it to us. He also promised that one day God will bring about a new world, free from evil, which will be even more wonderful than the one we know.

What can we do?

God's promise of a new world gives many people confidence to do all they can to fight against what is wrong and to make the world more as it should be.

Some work as scientists, trying to discover more about the world, and then put that knowledge to good use.

Some are in the world's governments, trying to see that the world's food and energy are shared out more fairly, and its wildlife protected.

Some are doctors, or teachers, or social workers, often going to the poorer countries of the world to give the people there a better way of life.

Some are parents trying to bring up children to make a better job of looking

We can help to make a better world by sharing with people in need.

We can share, not just food, but skills – bringing medical help to those who have no money to pay for it.

after the world when they grow up than others have in the past.

You do not have to wait until you are grown up to begin trying to make planet Earth a better place for all to live in.

Groups of children have cleared up untidy and neglected places to make pleasant places for play or rest.

Children can help plant baby trees. Their roots will stop the soil from being blown or washed away, and the land ruined.

Sometimes children organize events to raise money for good causes.

Children can visit elderly or sick people who are lonely, and help cheer them up.

We all have different interests, talents, and abilities. We should do all we can to develop and use them for the good of everyone, not just ourselves.

Facing the future

Many people are afraid of the future.

Will there be a nuclear war?

Will we run out of oil and coal and die of cold?

Could we pollute the earth so much that it can no longer support life?

Will there be another Ice Age?

Faced with these questions, it is good to have God's promise that because he loves and cares for his creation he is at work overcoming the evil in it and that one day there will be a new heaven and a new earth. We do not know exactly what this means, but we can reach out beyond ourselves to God who knows far more than we do, and with his help do all we can to treat this world and each other with love and care.

God's promise

'Then I saw a new heaven and a new earth, for the first heaven and the first earth had passed away . . . And I heard a loud voice from the throne saying, ''Now the dwelling of God is with men, and he will live with them. They will be his people, and God himself will be with them and be their God. He will wipe away every tear from their eyes. There will be no more death or mourning or crying or pain, for the old order of things has passed away.'' '

From the last book of the Bible: Revelation, chapter 21.

Index